Some Touches Are Not OK

By Nancy Kline and Karen Risech

Illustrated by Bonita Somers

FLOATING LEAF PRESS

FLOATING LEAF PRESS

Charlotte, North Carolina

A division of

WordPlay

Email: info@wordplaynow.com

www.wordplaynow.com

Library of Congress Control Number:2019916909

ISBN 978-1-950499-08-3

This book is dedicated to all children everywhere.
Karen, Bonita and Nancy are grandmothers,
and they hope that children will always speak up,
when and if needed, and that they will be
safe, nurtured and loved.

All children should know,
we want you to speak.
Don't hide any secrets!
It's your truth we seek.

Ever since you were a baby
you've loved hugs and kisses
smiling faces, new words
and gentle whispers.

Dad gives you loving hugs.

Mom tucks you in at night.

These are good touches,

and they feel so right.

Now you're running and jumping,
at home with Mom and Dad,
sharing stories from school —
Some are good. Some can be bad.

Grandma holds you on her lap
reading stories that rhyme.
You laugh together.
These times are sublime.

You have good friends.

You love them so much!

You play tag, share high fives —

these are both a good touch.

Someone might pull your hair,
fight, or push you in line.
You can use words to tell them
what they're doing's NOT fine.

If a touch ever hurts
or feels wrong to you,
that's a bad touch.
It's not right for you.

Don't kick a rabbit
or at birds throw a stone,
pull on a cat's tail,
or take a dog's bone.

We need to remember
animals are our friends.
We touch them nicely;
their love will never end.

A family party is usually fun,
so many relatives – what a bunch!
But some kisses can be yucky,
some hugs too big a crunch.

A touch shouldn't make you
feel sad or afraid.
Tell someone if ever
A bad touch is made.

Your body is private
from your head to your toes.
Don't let anyone touch you
in a way you oppose.

If it's a bad touch,
then say a strong, "NO!"
whether it's from a stranger
or someone you know.

You can tell adults you trust.

They want you to speak.

Don't hide secrets!

REMEMBER!

It's your truth they seek.

Authors' Photo by Anna Traylor

ABOUT THE AUTHORS

Nancy Kline grew up in Pennsylvania and graduated from Penn State University with a degree in journalism. She then worked as an editor in Philadelphia, before receiving certification in education. She taught grades K-3 before retiring, and now fills her time with reading, writing, yoga and walking. She cherishes her friends and family, which include three children, one grandchild and three rascally granddogs.

Karen Risech grew up on a farm in Illinois, attended St. Francis School of Nursing in Evanston, Illinois and later worked as a nurse on a Medical-Surgical Floor in Miami, Florida. She has four daughters and six grandchildren. Before retiring she worked for five years at a preschool in Miami. Her hobbies include book club, Mah Jongg, crafting and enjoying time with friends and family.

Even though Karen now lives in South Carolina, and Nancy lives in North Carolina, they live close to each other and spend time writing together.

ABOUT THE ILLUSTRATOR

Bonita Somers is an artist, teacher and the author/illustrator of the Ms. B's Art on a Cart book series designed for elementary aged students.

Bonita was born in Mason, Ohio and the second oldest of four siblings. After high school graduation she attended and received her Bachelor of Arts degree from Ohio's Bowling Green State University. With degree in hand and a secured job in San Antonio, TX, Bonita left the bitter winters for the warmth of Texas to begin a 20 year journey in the business world doing design and international purchasing work for wholesale florists and retail craft stores. She loved the opportunity to use her artistic skills while travelling the world. After her floral design and purchasing career she went back to school to get her teaching certificate to teach art. It was during this time that she jotted down her notes for her book series. Currently, Bonita is producing and teaching acrylic painting and alcohol ink art in the Charlotte, NC area.

Bonita's philosophy on art is not to take anything too seriously. Have fun, learn, and enjoy the process. You are never going to "arrive". So, keep learning and pay your knowledge forward.

For more information on Bonita's art, books, and class schedules visit: **www.BoSomers.com**.

Made in the USA
Monee, IL
25 March 2025